The Shaping of Me

Lisa Scovell-Strickland

ME

Every day I play a different role
Not sharing what's deep within my soul
I watch as people judge my strengths
They dig and delve, go to any lengths
But whom can I trust? When will they see?
Who I really am, the secret me

Published by
Lemon Jelly Press
Isle of Wight
UK
PO30 5HY

www.lemonjellypress.co.uk

ISBN 978-191-6021-440

Cover design by Charlotte Begg

Acknowledgements

For me, myself and I as I finally realise that am I not broken, just healing.

I acknowledge all those who have come into my life and added to its tapestry.

I particularly want to thank:

Zara for loving me, when I couldn't love myself

Annette and Darren for being my constant supporters, especially when I cannot believe in myself

Charlotte, for joining me on this journey and guiding me through it all with patience and encouragement

The cameo stranger, whose kind words gave me the confidence to break free of my insecurities to believe that this was not only possible but that my words are beautiful.

WHY I LAY BARE MY HEART

I see your eyes questioning me silently
A flicker of worry at your brow
You pose the questions I've been waiting for
Why? You ask
What made you choose this path?
I inhale slowly, wanting to get my words just right
I am doing this to heal myself
To lift the weight holding me down
To quell the darkness deep inside
To remove the shackles I dressed myself in
To carve out a future on my own terms
And along the way I hope to bring light to others in the darkness
As I show them that they are not alone
That the darkness can be overcome
That they too can become a phoenix

CONTENTS

THE SHAPING OF ME

The childhood that shaped me
Taught me excessive regulation of my daily intake
Because I have to maintain my waistline

Instilled in me a sense of lacking
I lacked height, beauty and popularity
Because being loyal and kind wasn't enough

Created in me an obsessive need for control
Of my true narrative, who I was, whom I told
Because not everyone understood the real me

Developed in me a deep self-loathing
Those popular boys whispering sweet nothings with hands where they shouldn't be
Because you can be unpopular but used all the same

ALL THE WAYS I TRIED TO EASE MY PAIN

Once the pain inside got too much
I had to let it all out
So I tried to cut it free
But that just bought more pain
And the evidence was difficult to hide

Next, I tried to purge myself
Pushed my fingers down inside
But my throat said no thank you
Besides I'd only eaten an apple all day
I hadn't thought this through

Then I tried to scream it all away
I closed my eyes, hands over my ears
Looking skywards I tried to roar
The sound only filled my head
And my ears were ringing for days

Again I sought to restrict myself
I picked and prodded each meal
An apple and a chocolate bar a day
Were all I allowed myself
Even restriction was losing its charm

So instead I took up my pen
Wrote down random words to start
Quickly sentences appeared
Thoughts, feelings, desires, shame, fears, darkness
It all started to pour out of me
Sometimes in rhyme, mostly in blank verse
And every so often in streams of consciousness

With each word I wrote
I felt the weight lift
The pain ease
My inner self revive
Now I fear the day I run out of words

CONSENT

At the club with my friends to dance away
You singled me out, I became your prey
In my quest for hedonism to set me free
I failed to realise your beady eyes on me

Get off, get back
I didn't say yes to that

I lost my words with that last shot downed
You stalked me all over your hunting ground
You trapped me in that corner, in the dark
Your rough touch sought to dim my spark

Get off, get back
I didn't say yes to that

I tried to struggle as you hand climbed my thigh
I couldn't fight you off, I determined not to cry
I am reminded that you are not the first one
All those others who've tried to have their little fun

Get off, get back
I didn't say yes to that

I come to my senses, I find my fight
You've had your thrill, disappear from my sight

Get off, get back
I didn't say yes to that

I collect myself, smooth my dress
I try to forget your unwanted caress
I search for safety, fight my distress
I want to forget this god awful mess

As I find myself home
In the shower on my own
I whisper in the spray
One day I'll be ok
Why couldn't I speak
Why was I so weak
All I wanted to say

Get off, get back
No I don't consent to that

SELF-CONTROL

Now I want you to listen good
To a story about me and food
I started young
And so, I begun
To see what inches, I could lose
To keep up with the other girl's views
Of how I should look
Like that model in that book
They teased me as I was already thin
I felt the pressure, they got under my skin
No breakfast, lunch or dinner
Cause I wanted to be a winner
Keeping their "friendship" was my prize
Little did I know that they coveted my size
It wasn't about me, but all about them
Their jealousy set out to condemn
I starved myself for their little games
The punishing cycle in me still remains
And sometimes I still use that self-control
An engrained need to restrict me to feel whole

STONE

My sharp corners don't really come to much
Sitting, staying, being all yet nothing
I wish I could be extrovert
I wish I could be a laugh
I am neither, I am cold, I am me
I am nothing worth talking about
When they call out names, mine is nothing special
I have a few curves and that is all
Being interesting is something I cannot afford
I am one out of millions, but you won't bother me
I am not spicy enough
I am plain monotone

INTO TEMPTATION

Into the open arms of him, I ran
Into temptation, I went with this man
Knowing the consequences, I went on
Knowing the ending, I played along

Clichés of old he delivered, I fell
His secrets lost, only lies he could sell
A sparkle in his eye, me in his Nile
His gem for tonight, I was caught in his smile

Into the open arms of this great man
Into temptation, nirvana I ran
Into his open arms, he pierced my heart
Into temptation and his scripted part

THE DESTRUCTION OF A WOMAN

Brick by brick he pulled my defences down
It wasn't like falling, it was like drowning, slowly
Each missing brick took away my strength
Out of need or out of love did he do it?
He treated me well to everyone's surprise
His hypnotic smile had already conquered
Why should he treat me any different?
But it was the plan, he always used seduction
He quite liked it
I know I did
It didn't take long, the cement had only just been laid
I thought I was strong, I guess I was weak
Ensnared in his arms I thought I was safe
Love hides many demons from the world
Charmed by his spells
Enslaved by his passion until the end
With all my defences gone I died inside

WHISPERS

Your touch burns my skin
  As it renders me silent
    But it will not leave any marks
      It will be the whispering words
        That bind me to you
          The sweet nothings
            That trap me into your embrace
            The staccato of your cadence
              That cuts deep, leaving chronic wounds
              I find my way into my gilded cage
                Locking the door from the inside
                Kneeling in servitude
                  Waiting for your whispering
                  Diatribe to set me free

UNDER THE CONTROL OF OTHERS

I am not sure when I had noticed
Not sure when I could tell
I'd found myself situated
In some kind of quiet hell

My world all closed in upon itself
Its boundaries wound round me tight
I've been trying to extend them for so long
Exhaustion sapping from me my fight

All my frames of reference focused to the right
Tied to a life that wasn't mine
My connections snuffed out one by one
Each loss occurred within slow time

As I take in the hollowed self of me
I realise how much of me has been taken
Or was it that I let myself fade away
I now promise to myself that I will not be forsaken

NUMB

Falling downward like heavy rain
Bits and pieces of me
Splash across each surface
Messy and randomly spread
I tried to create order and routine
To hide my pain
Ease my burdens
A glamour for my humdrum numb
Now you find me incomplete
Aching to fulfil my potential
Struggling to find my way out
Rather than lend me your hand
I turn and see you lock me in
Weakly protesting
I sink again
Another opportunity missed for respite
As I sit amongst the ashes, reflecting
I wonder how I find myself here
My silent scream burns

I awake to ground hog day
Again
And
Again
And
Again

Grant me the courage to start anew
Bestow on me strength in my voice
Show me the way to my truth

STREAM OF EMOTION

Spiralling out of control – out of mind – out of body – clinging to the whisper of my soul – a bitter sweet wind tests my resolve and asks me to dance the last tango – I decline preferring to sit amongst the wall flowers – slowly fading away – slipping in and out of consciousness – my resolve spiralling in the bottom of an empty glass – my mind in and out and going crazy – numbness set in last June but I have only just started to notice – little words spoken softly and served up with sarcasm – did I see this coming? – or was it the moment I stepped into the eye and the words spun around me? – anti-clockwise as I recall – but I'm crazy – branded for all to see but I keep it well hidden – except now the mystery has been shattered and I am laying myself bare for all to see.

INSOMNIA

Wide awake again tonight
Bolt upright at half past one
My hands clutching my throat
The memory of rough hands lingers
My shallow breaths stutter painfully
My heart pounds through all of me
A screeching metronome out of sync
I caught in a fugue state, eyes glazed
Counting back from ten
Desperate to gain control
I berate myself for such weakness
Over that experience from so long again
My pulse slows, I feel myself return
I wait for sleep, hoping for better dreams to come

MUTE

I am full of emotions, thoughts and opinions
They dwell within me locked up tight
Each time I try to release one
I feel cotton balls stuck in my throat
Stuffing my syntax back into me to hide its meaning
The words I rehearse over
and over
Perfect the script I want to voice
But as the moment arrives
Earth fills my mouth burying my tongue
I choke on everything I wished to convey
And when it really matters for me to state my case
I tilt my head to release my locution
Whilst my tongue forms each syllable
Even in a scream there is
silence
I find my hand over my mouth
Realising that I have
no sound,
no agency no expression
I am mute
tied by my own fears and the overbearance of
others

LOST TO MYSELF

As the nib of my pen begins each word
I struggle to find myself
I look in all the right places
But there is no trace of me
I look for the smile that used to shine
I search for the gold in my eyes
I watch for the sway of my dancing hips
But they do not reveal themselves
I am lost in my head
I am all at sea
I stare into empty eyes
Full of cynicism
Full of longing
Full of bruised hope
I shine a light on what I once was
Desperate to reignite myself
Slowly I see the sparks stutter
Getting brighter with each strike
I nurse the embers
Please let them catch
For I want to see those flames again
Feel the heat of untold desires
See the world through the light of my smile
And watch as I burn brightly
To lead others from the darkness

THE IMPACT OF YOUR WORDS

I wish you could see things
The way I feel them
Hear the words you pour out
A constant stream of deprecation
When I ask you to review them
You retort that they are witticisms
But all I hear are pointed criticisms
Layer upon layer they come
Landing at the heart of me
Weakening my resolve
My confidence
Striking at the last vestiges
Of my soul
I crack open
My insecurity and sadness breaking forth
I snap towards you
Desperate to fight my corner
It's wasted as always
As everything is twisted
Back in your favour
So to protect myself
I become muted
Inward
And despondent

WARRIOR

I learn to defend myself
Against your negativity
Each blow cuts quick
My usual counter and strike rendered useless
Whilst I had developed my skills
Strengthened my muscles
I find myself bought to my knees
Your words bind me in chains
I remember that I too have words
And I relearn to use them
To create distraction, deflection
I become the word warrior that you were not expecting
Fighting my corner with my truth vocabulary

SELF-CONTROL REVISITED

I have learnt to love myself a little
To let go of the strict control of my waistline
However, now I have new ways…
To restrict myself
To punish myself
I sink into myself
Drowning in my own self-loathing
Over analysing…
Every interaction
Every word spoken
Every thought manifested
The swirling crescendo of all my negativity
Rushes through every particle of me
Sticking tightly to my synapses
Forming a cerebral muscle memory
Engraining self-sabotage
Which now comes as easy as breathing
And I am oh so exasperated by it all

MIRROR, MIRROR ON THE BATHROOM WALL

I try
to love you
unconditionally /
celebrate your flaws
alongside your grace / see your
beauty wild and untamed / but
as I look in the mirror / all I see are
the failures laid bare /
hear the criticisms ringing aloud /
feel the self-loathing course
through me / tomorrow I will
change this I say / realising
that I said this yesterday /
and all the days
before

EQUILIBRIUM

Yesterday I was on a high
Today I have fallen to a low
Last Wednesday I was in between
My fickle equilibrium is failing me
It mocks me daily, refuses to balance
When I think that I'm on a streak of calm
It rears its ugly head to face me
Challenging me to a duel
Handing me a loaded gun
Filled with bullets of anxiety, fear, regret and doubt
I reach for my armour of happiness
Hoping to be strapped in tight
Before the gun is cocked
I close my eyes, take a deep breath
Whispering my special song to myself
As the shot is fired, ringing in my ears
I find that this time happiness won
My affirmations held fast
And I turn to start the day

QUIET

Outwardly quiet I sit still without emotion
Fixated on the book shelf in the non-fiction section
Following the librarian's directions
Momentarily I forget what I am looking for
The torrent of emotions wage war inside my mind
Yet to those around me I am a picture of calm
Steadily scouring the shelves for that book I just have to read
My internal library runs amok
Flicking through the microfiche of my past
Replaying old scenarios and headlines I wish forgotten
Something snaps and I scream with all I have
Gasping for breath, I brace myself
Opening my eyes I expect to have caused a scene
However, no one looks and I realise
That all anyone can see is my fingers
On the spine of the book I was looking for all along

RE-WRITING THE NARRATIVE

I want to peel away my skin
To look beneath
To find out why I feel this way
Why I cannot hold onto happiness for long
As I reach for a button labelled self-destruct
If I could see right inside
Poke around the dark corners
Question my sinew and bones
Travel along my synapses
Would I find the answer?
If I crawled into my heart
Felt each beat from the inside
Would I find the key?
A way to smooth the wrinkles of emotion
From the vast peaks and valleys that I travel across
I think I would discover that it all comes back to my grey matter
That those engrained muscle memory synapses are the cause
That have set and affirmed my negative patterns
Years of dark mantras voiced by others
That slowly became my own
Once I realise this

I can change this
I can rewrite the narrative
I can create my affirmations
I can reclaim myself
I can smooth my wrinkled emotions
I can believe in me

AM I BROKEN?

I sit down to write about the beautiful
The happiness and the colourful
But as the pen hits the paper
My mood reverses and out pours the angst
The darkness, uncertainty and anxiety
That bubbles beneath the surface of my being
I turn the page and try again
Futility reigns as my disquiet pushes through
Am I really this broken, beyond repair?
Will I ever learn to turn the tide on my pain?
As I take a break to contemplate
I see the sun's rays stretch towards me
Forcing back the shadow of myself
The corners of my mouth climb upwards
As I realise the tide has already turned
With each word that I put down

I vanquish the darkness
I relinquish the angst
I reverse the uncertainty
I starve the anxiety
I am no longer broken
I am just starting to heal

BANISHING THE VOICE IN MY HEAD

The voice in my head
It sits right at the back
In the darkness
All alone
                Cutting an imposing presence
                I try not to listen
                To plug my ears
                But it has a direct line
A permanent feed
A stream of negativity
Wearing me down
Stealing the joy
                Minimising my achievements
                What makes it so awful
                Is that it is version of me I thought I had banished
                But sometimes I resurrect it
Court it's presence
Feed it my anxiety
I decry myself at once and scream
Be gone, stay away
I don't want to listen to you today, tomorrow, or ever again
                I blink thrice
                Casting my mind to search
                For the darkness in me
                Finding nothing, I click the lock in place
                And this time throw away the key

SEEN

Today I felt truly seen
Through a computer screen, a stranger's cameo
She interpreted my emotions as requested
Reading my prepared lines aloud
In such a beautiful and unexpected way
I felt naked, but so understood
I cried tears of absolution
As I felt my past and present
Echoed in her own narrative
I realised the interpretation of my words
Will be the healing balm I have always searched for
As I give voice to the darkness, happiness, sadness and uncertainty of others
Through each line that pours from the heart of me

DEAR DIARY...ABOUT TODAY

Dear diary...about today
Not sure how to frame this
Boy, I have a lot to say

If I focus on the negativity
Not sure I'd have room
Cause it's my favoured proclivity

So, I'd like to try something new
A little experiment
To consider a different view

I'd like to focus on all the good
To reframe my narrative
To remember what I withstood

So, I list what went the right way
The positive interactions
What had me smiling away

I realise I've flipped it all on its head
With a list of successes
I finally look forward to tomorrow instead

THE HIDDEN ME

I learnt to hide the real me
Lock it away tight for safe keeping
I'd known those who were open
Witnessing their daily struggles
The actions of others too often unkind
Fear and loathing preventing kindness and acceptance
The more I locked myself in
The more I faded away
A shadow of myself
Letting others take me for granted
When I should have guarded my heart
Fortified my mind, withheld my body
I existed in a world I had created meant to please others
A public show of perfect
One day the cracks began to show
A match was lit
I stepped out of the flames
Reborn in the sparkle of the rainbow
Ready to start again

WORDS

Today I saw the impact of my words
The way my gratitude touched their core
And I remind myself that words matter
The words that drape around you like a warm hug
The ones which lift you up when you are at your lowest
The mean ones which destroy your confidence over time
The bitter words meant to cause maximum pain again and again
And the words that ring in your head round and around on constant replay, a
mantra that's either good or evil
I hope that my words always land in the right place, at the right time
Words matter greatly to me
I hope that I always choose them carefully

NEW BEGINNINGS

New book, new beginnings
To the bitter end of it all
My sweet sorrow
A testament to love
Looking from the inside out
To time immemorial
The middle of the road
To purgatory and back
Innocence renews it vows
Father time makes love to mother earth
Seasons beckon to a compromise
As remembrance sighs again
A new day breaks once more
And memories fade to grey

VULNERABILITY

With every word I write
I strip myself bare to my bones
So you can see into the heart of me
With each beat, my secrets pour out
My truths sent out into the ether
I'm trusting you with the essence of me
This vessel filled to the brim with vulnerability
Along with my shame, my guilt
My darkness and my happiness
They shape the very fibre of me
My spirit once riven, now salutary
Should you wish to bear me ill intent
Proceed carefully, my redoubt is unyielding these days
Should you wish to bear me only goodwill
I pledge to be your steadfast ally
For as long as you keep me in your good graces

PHOENIX

Forged from the fires within
I rest in the ashes
Ready to spread my wings
I bide my time, testing my potential
Building my resilience, taming my disquiet
Those tentative first steps become purposeful
As I rise above the ashes I made
I am reborn
I am determined
I am truth
And I will be my own legacy

I become unstoppable
A divine resilience

See me
Revere me
For I am glorious

A LOVE LETTER TO THE GIRL I USED TO BE

Dear Me,

I remember a slip of a girl
Long dark brown hair, hazel eyes
All toothy smiles and vibrant
Full of life but unsure of the world
Led by others
Needing to please
Determined to be loved by all

I wish I could tell her she was enough
That she was exactly as she was meant to be
To let her know that the important people love her unconditionally
That all others are just peripheral on her journey through this world
I ache to tell her that the pain won't last forever
To hold on to her truths and one day they will be accepted without rejection

Above all, I want to tell her that I love her inside and out
Although at times I was lost to her
At times it was difficult to feel that love
On the worst days that it turned to hate
I never gave up hope, I never lost that love really

Now I cherish that love
I fuel it daily
I accept all the negativity
I celebrate all the positivity
And bear witness to all that's in between
Dear girl, I have always loved you
And now I get to show you everyday
As I love myself, in spite of myself
And those around me
This has become another of my truths
Never forget that

Love Me

STANDING ON THE EDGE OF SOMETHING NEW

I stand here on the edge of everything I hold dear
One leap of faith away from new beginnings
I reflect on where I have come from
As I lay myself bare for all to see
All my fears, regrets and pain set out in lines
All my hopes and dreams just starting to grace the pages
I have come further than I thought possible
The first steps were the most clumsy
The second steps were emboldened
The next steps will be the test
Of my own resilience, will it sustain?
Of those I hold dear, who will catch me if I fall?
Of new eyes, who will stand in judgement?
I hold my head high, my eyes closed
My toes overhang that narrow ledge
A deep breath to centre myself
A tear to grieve for what I leave behind

A smile as I see what I can achieve
I open my eyes
Unfurl my wings
Bending my knees

I

       take

              that

                     leap

Faith lifting me to new heights
Courage helping me soar
Destiny plotting a course for something beautiful
I realise that I was a phoenix all along
Just waiting to be reborn at the right time
I see sunrise on the horizon, realising
The perfect timing was this moment from the beginning

Ingram Content Group UK Ltd.
Milton Keynes UK
UKHW020216170723
425191UK00009B/102

9 781916 021440